Vanishing Horizon

ANHINGA PRESS

Also by Gerry LaFemina

Poetry

Rest Stops (1989)

23 Below (1994)

The City of Jazz and Punk (1995)

Shattered Hours: Poems 1988-1994 (1997)

A Print of Wildflowers (1997)

Zarathustra in Love (2001)

A Garment Sewn from Night Itself (2003)

Graffiti Heart (2003)

The Window Facing Winter (2004)

The Parakeets of Brooklyn (2005)

*Figures from The Big Time Circus Book/
The Book of Clown Baby* (2007)

Translation
Voice Lock Puppet: Poems of Ali Yuce
(with Sinan Toprak) (2002)

Fiction
Wish List: Stories (2009)

Anthologies

Poetry 30 (edited with Daniel Crocker) (2005)

*Evensong: Contemporary American Poets
on Spirituality* (edited with Chad Prevost) (2006)

Token Entry: Odes to the New York Subway (2011)

Vanishing Horizon

Poems

Gerry LaFemina

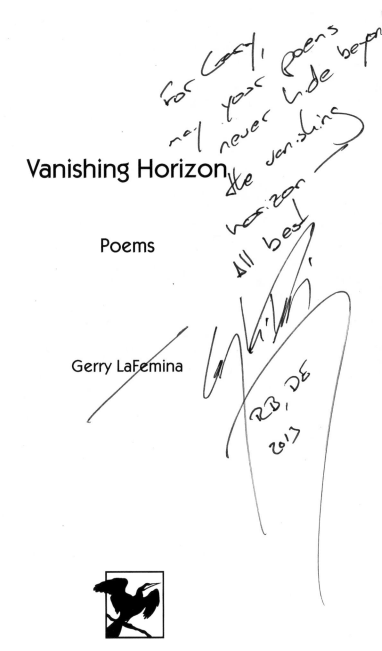

For Gary,
may your poems
never hide beyond
the vanishing
horizon
All best
RB, DE
2013

ANHINGA PRESS
TALLAHASSEE, FLORIDA 2011

Cover art: *STILL* by Beth Piver, 24" x 18" acrylic on canvas
Author photograph: Curtis Tompkins
Cover/Text Design: Jill Runyan
Type Styles: titles set in Kabel Medium and text set in Minion Pro

Library of Congress Cataloging-in-Publication Data
Vanishing Horizon by Gerry LaFemina – First Edition
ISBN – 978-1-934695-22-7
Library of Congress Cataloging Card Number – 2010938012

Anhinga Press Inc. is a nonprofit corporation dedicated wholly to the publication and appreciation of fine poetry and other literary genres.

For personal orders, catalogs
and information write to:
Anhinga Press
P.O. Box 3665
Tallahassee, Florida 32315
Web site: www.anhinga.org
E-mail: info@anhinga.org

Published in the United States
by Anhinga Press
Tallahassee, Florida
First Edition, 2011

In memory of Stella Misiara, 1919-2010

Contents

Acknowledgments

I want to thank the editors of the following magazines for previously publishing some of these poems:

5 a.m.: "The Hawk & Its Shadow Fly the Same Pattern" and "Although I've Stopped Believing in Miracles"

Artful Dodge: "After Reading Rexroth I Step Outside"

Asheville Poetry Review: "Maybe in Syncopated Time"

Beltway Poetry Quarterly: "Poem Found in the Graffiti on a Freight Train's Cars"

Big City Lit: "While Listening to Burning Spear, I Remember Sherry and her Father" and "Storm Front, Moving East"

Broadkill Review: "Upper East Side, Winter 2002"

Caribbean Writer: "From a Room Overlooking the Beach"

Chatahoochee Review: "Returning Home in the MG Just Before Dawn"

Connecticut Review: "Treatise on the Possibility of a God of Love"

Controlled Burn: "Cooking Italian"

The Cortland Review: "The Sacrosanct"

Crab Orchard Review: "Go Hawaiian"

Gargoyle: "No Omen"

Gettysburg Review: "Contact Points," "Perspective, St. Thomas, USVI," and "One Bird Feeder Feeds at Least Four Dozen Birds"

McSweeney's: "The Silence that Follows"

New Works Review: "Cold Sun Over Queens," "Walking the Neighborhood the Morning after a Snowstorm," and "Zen Relativity"

No Tell Motel: "The Lost Love Letters of Cumberland," "Train Whistle Far from Town, Approaching," and "January 1, 2008"

North American Review: "After Breakfast I Consider String Theory," "Alphabet City," and "Perfidia"

Patterson Literary Review: "Perspective: New York City"

Pleiades: "Poem Found Among Scraps of a Lower East Side Gutter"

Ratapallax: "Saint Sparrow"

Redactions: "Fire Engine, Early Morning"
Shenandoah: "A Kind of Holiness"
The Southeast Review: "Calabash," "Manchineel," "Mango,"
     "Papaya," and "Soursop & Oranges"
Temenos: "Phenomenology of the Vanishing Horizon"
Willow Springs: "Elegy for my 34th Year"

"Returning Home in the MG, Just Before Dawn" received a Pushcart
Prize and appeared in *Pushcart Prize XXXIII: Best of the Small Presses,*
2009 Edition.

"The Silence that Follows" appears in *With a Cherry on Top*, Angela
Williams and Judith Kerman, eds, published by Mayapple Press. It
also appears in the *McSweeney's Book of Poets Picking Poets*, Dominic
Luxford, ed, published by McSweeney's.

"The Sacrosanct" appears in *Come Together, Imagine Peace*, Philip
Metres, Ann Smith and Larry Smith, eds, published by Bottom Dog
Press, 2008.

"Thinking of the Franciscan Abbey after Reading James Wright"
and "My Father Watching my Mother Shaving" appear in *Detroit:
Stories*, Peter Markus, ed, published by Museum of Contemporary
Art Detroit, 2009.

"Phenomenology of the Vanishing Horizon" appears in *Breathe:
Contemporary Odes*, Chad Prevost and Ryan VanCleave, eds,
published by C&R Press, 2009.

The epigraph is from Michael Burkard's "The Mysteries of Things"
which appears in his book, *The Fires They Kept*.

Vanishing Horizon

These are just a few things
which have constantly followed me:
the sun, the moon,
many many stars,
night, day,
streets, even the streets of this metropolis, streets
which truly seem to lead into absolutely
nowhere, especially in rain ...
— *Michael Burkard*

Returning Home in the MG Just Before Dawn

The last rags of cloud have dispersed
displaying the harvest moon's mandala burnished,
but seeming as far away
                as a saxophone

a friend retired four years ago,
the one she sometimes pulls from the closet — not to play,
but rather to hear the reedy echo of song
lodged in its long esophagus.

Imagine that song is a hymn.
Imagine it is sung by a famished cat on the front porch.

Imagine it's sung by vibrations of the last struck chord
on that stand-up piano shoved in grandmother's living room corner;

sung by the engine at 4000 RPM;
sung by the grackle right before dawn.

How soon I return to the rind of this world —
the misgivings of sparrows & neighbor kids who wake
with my arrival; the lawn laminated with dew;

my house barren, shut down like a stage
but for the porch light

which brightens a spider's safety net
stretched tightly between two skeletal limbs of birch.

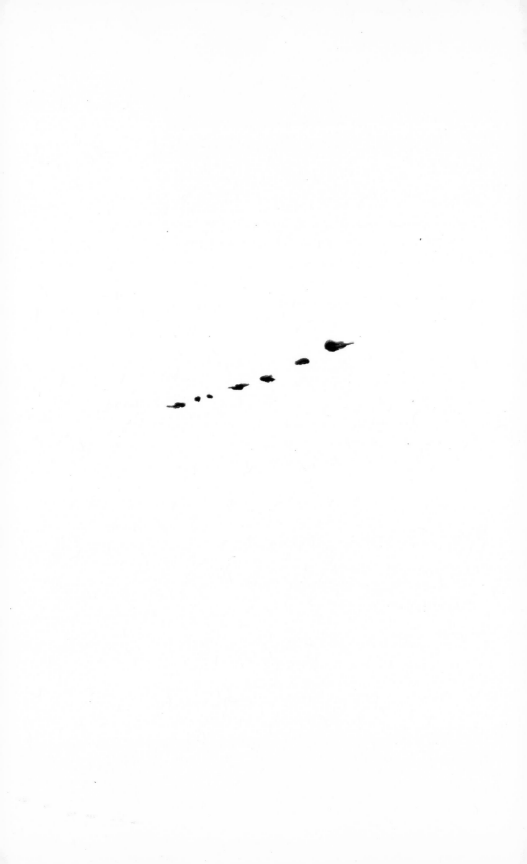

Although I've Stopped Believing in Miracles

On the night of my birth, the Pleiades meteors
wore their iridescent capes over Bensonhurst, where

nobody could see them, &

really my mother wasn't thinking of the heavens at all
beyond a grateful prayer that she'd given birth again
to a healthy child. All the while
my dad dealt hand after hand of seven card stud
in the waiting room with three orderlies, a janitor, & one more

father-to-be;
                    a transistor radio crackled with crowd sounds —
a Mets game deep in the eighth inning.
                              Did my mother want
to name me after the dead president's assassinated brother?
Maybe she would have
                    if it weren't also my father's name.

I was born into a time of riots, when nobody looked toward the sky.

Nearly 40 years later & little is different,
which suggests one thing my father says might be right: *Gerard,*
the more things change, the more they stay the same.
Though I hate to think so
                    despite another story
about a woman surprised she'd just given birth;
she'd always had an erratic period, she insisted.

She never claimed it impossible, but never mentioned
a boyfriend or husband. Still,
I'll assume there was a father because I've long stopped believing

in miracles. This isn't meant to sound cynical. I don't fathom
everything has a rational answer
                              because in Brooklyn
crowds are gathering at an underpass of the Giwanis

where a water stain is said to resemble the Virgin Mary.
Thus a makeshift shrine has been established —
glass ensconced wicks flickering lower into liquid wax
& lilies slowly losing their large white petals so

in the wind of passing traffic
                              they disperse
like playing cards. So many people hold vigil there

& others stop just to pray briefly — some genuflect like birds,
& even that group of young men coming back from stickball …
they've taken off their ball caps,
                              which sag now in their hands.

They look toward the puddles & are surprised by their reflections.
They say little to each other, astonished by what they've gotten to see
in this hollow beneath a highway
                              within that well-lit city.

No Omen

I open the office door &
there's a crow — black as slicked back hair & as shiny

ascending from the file cabinet toward the fluorescent fixture.

All weekend it must've shifted in its impatience
from desk to bookcase to the screenless window I'd closed last Friday.
Feather tufts scattered.
                    All weekend
it fluttered & cawed & pecked among the books & papers
— desperate.

                There was that time
I locked myself in three chord punk rock
the singers angry & angrier —
                        how they cawed & cawed.

That long late August my heart was a crow. No:
those weeks my heart felt like it had been pecked out.

There was a girl,
                of course, & music …
More immediately, though, there is this crow,

wings spread, annoyed.
                    I won't pretend it showed up here
to teach me something, won't look for meaning
in all its magnificent fury,
for how can I understand the wisdom of crows?

Instead I try to name the crow — call it Brother,
call it Corvus. Call it padre or Apollo.

Call it Gerard as if it were my alter ego,
but the crow just stays near the ceiling, so I look at it
the way I saw my mother with her concern in silhouette

at the top of the stair.
What I thought was love was an empty office I went to,
the work of which I didn't understand,

        still don't,

but the crow is just a crow &

I know enough now to open the window & wait
until that lone bird flies toward the breeze,
its wings rattling the window frame once,

twice so it hesitates

      before finding finally its way.

I don't care to watch it shrink into a black speck
against the spring sky,

      but I'll collect the bouquet of feathers
it dropped one petal at a time, & save them
in clear plastic kept in my desk,

know they're there like the darkened photographs
of my old self, hair dyed jet, gelled back, my arm
around the waist of a young woman who already looks away.

The Lost Love Letters of Cumberland

I know she wrote them — Shawnda —
but don't know (can't know, really) whether he read them.
If not, did she just misplace these folded sheets of looseleaf —

her chubby, cursive declarations of love — or
did she leave them deliberately there

like square-winged moths on a bench downtown
slightly ruffling in the slight wind.

There are, of course, some answers I can never know

though I try to picture Andrew's pimpled, bemused face
& close-cropped hair
not knowing if this urge when he's around her
to touch her is love

or something … baser. He's sixteen after all
so why wouldn't he throw away those notes
that proclaim, *I wanna be with you*
for the rest of my life until I die. I wanna have your kids?

I can't say but there they were
some with a lingering patina of perfume, & I gathered them up
gently, fingering each sheet

so I could fold them up perfectly again
as if they had never been read
                              even though I had no intention
of returning them. Hadn't I thrown away
all the romantic notes of my youth

— the ones I wrote & never sent,
the one I didn't receive?

A girl I loved then committed suicide & another
was born again;
                   & Shawnda
looks downward all the time & complains bitterly to
her friends. I've seen

her or someone just like her at the shopping mall & coffee shop.
It always comes back to Andrew
who does what he always does

& who seems confused by her crying
& who says to her, *I love you* & hopes he means it,

& who is like any of us in the face of that overwhelming.

Zen Relativity

Then a downpour rinsed, finally, the cinders from the streets,
cinders the road crews had spread on March snow
to induce melting.
               Now a fine sediment of soot on everything

after the eventual thaw, eventual evaporation.

If only enlightenment were so easy:

my cat asleep on the softest spot she could find —
a basket of clean laundry, jeans & shirts stacked high;
mint tea in its Japanese pot, steeping,

two cups patient … Lester Young's saxophone unraveling
in another room; Voltaire's collected letters dog-eared to

"On Infinity & Chronology."
What is time if not a way to create some hierarchy
of trespasses & forgiveness? All hour

                              that saxophone
& rain like 10,000 ticks of a stopwatch simultaneously.

For some, god's a pillar of cloud in the desert; for some,
god's the mystery of relativity,
that equation where time slows nearer the speed of light.

I pour the tea. In its dissipating steam,
the sublime or something like it.

Cooking Italian

From the kitchen: scent of peppers broiling
until the skin bubbles & blackens & can be easily removed.

If this is what temperature does to flesh,
it's no wonder the body can be reduced to ash, bone
fragments & tooth enamel after the crematorium

while photographs of old loves just curl, transform
into trash can embers.
                              Of course there's the phoenix myth
but that does most of us no good in this age of reason.

I learned how to roast peppers & tomatoes from Frances,
who'd pat my cheek when I'd see her

in my cousin's kitchen. I was nearly thirty
& hadn't had a grandmother in a long time …

During Frances's service I cooked in her honor,
nearly 700 miles from where her remains were scattered.
I ate the veggies hot
                              with olive oil infused with garlic,

the tastes skating my tongue
even as the roof of my mouth scorched.

Eating should be like being in love, she advised.

There was wine & water, surely, on the table
though the house was empty of even a chance
of transubstantiation.

I thought of those monks
in scarlet garb stepping on hot coals
& of the woman I believed I loved,

then forked more of that spicy pulp into my mouth.

Papaya

Perhaps the heart is more like a papaya —
it takes a large knife to split it
& we could eat its pink meat

but only after we've scooped its black seeds
mucousy like spawn
which we leave on a small plate. Later

the hard green husk remains, left
leathery as a sadness,
as the memory of a sadness.

My Father Watching My Mother Shaving

— After Dennis Hinrichsen

The water no longer poured from the faucet,
so he must not have known
she was in there when he opened the bathroom door.

What surprise —
                                her leg out of the water.
Did he look askance, mumbling

some apology allowing her to glimpse momentarily
the small boy he once was? Probably
he just stood in the doorway, unmovable, & stared.

He was home late from cards, cigarette smoke
lathered into his fingers,
                                & she had wearied of waiting.

How did she react —
cool air entering all that steam? Did she flinch slightly

& thus cut herself below the left knee,
three drops of red falling into the water & blooming
into liquid carnations? Perhaps

my father rose to the occasion right then
& knelt beside the tub, ripped

a piece of tissue the way he'd do
if he'd cut his chin in the morning, & pressed it
against her small wound.

I have to believe there was still this possibility

for tenderness so near the end.
Picture them there, they're almost
strangers: my 30-year old mother in the bath,
a razor in her hand, her leg water-glazed,

& my father, a few months older, on his knees
seemingly penitent as in our rooms my brother, sister & I slept.

Lullaby for my Mother

My mother sleeps deeply now
but back when I would sing "American Pie" &
"All you Need is Love" from the backseat of our Plymouth Duster,
the streets of Brooklyn were puddled with the rain
that always seemed to streak the windows of that car
so that now, when I remember it, Bensonhurst is just a blur.
Back then she'd wake easily — at the slightest creak

of a floorboard or at the sigh of the ice box door.
Even though she sleeps deeply now,
how many times had she caught me in that
temporary light, some leftover drumstick in my hand
for the hunger that always haunted me,
the way she was haunted by her anger.
What did I know of the risks that come with love?

She'd shake her head then retreat to her bedroom
where she kept her sadnesses in a bureau drawer.
They had killed Kennedy & King right
before I was born, & still she held hope,
but then my father left & loneliness
became a horizon — long & impossible to get beyond.
This was how I learned to sing with the radio

though never "Cats in the Cradle …," which I still won't
sing because now my mother sleeps deeply.
Some days she called us three kids together so
we could eat dinner together in the apartment
we'd just moved to or would soon move from.
The chicken slightly burnt & dry with Shake-N-Bake
that we all agreed — for what else could we say — tasted delicious.

Poem Composed in the Alphabet of Bats

All night I counted the rain's footsteps
as it prowled these streets; now, sleep
still creeps by our bed like a cat. In the space between storm

& daybreak's magenta glare I hear filmy wings & know
the bats hunt crickets & moths. Come sun up

they'll have merged with whatever darkness they can find

the way I once hoped to vanish
into music: into power chords from a pawn-shop Telecaster
or into the full exhalation of a tenor saxophone.

Any test I might've taken then I couldn't pass
even though I knew how
the breath of a woman is a type of music.
                                        I can hear it
in the caesuras overheard in restaurants.

In the back pew of churches, the widows whisper their rote prayers.

The priest who longed to live in a sacristy of silence
says little; when he recites scripture
each word seems a hornet in his mouth. Who doesn't love his sermons?
five minutes of quiet,

not even a sore throat in complaint.

Lord, accept my insomnia as a sacrifice.
My woman snores the mantra of fitful sleep. It calls *follow   follow.*

Rain & low clouds outside — our streets blur into mist

but nothing's gone for good:
haven't we all seen the magician's assistant reappear.

So, let's toast poor Thomas who trusted nothing but his own
senses: the feel of that blood against his fingertips …

Then he lifted those plasma-gowned fingers to his lips.

In the front's wake, the residual fog will disperse, reveal
retired water heaters & sinks in the yard of my plumber neighbor.

At 89, most days he's off in his pick-up with pipes & tools
working for the widows of Grayling.
                                        He asks no pay
but once he was given a daughter's old burnished saxophone.
George doesn't play.

Still he keeps its brass well-polished & displays its young girl's neck.

Sometimes we can hear the high school band marching
in the distance, a poltergeist of melody filtering through the plaster

so vague we're not sure if we've actually heard it

until they're done.

                          Or else it's the National Guard again,
practicing artillery.
The shells like a coming storm that never arrives

I want to walk into rain & be gone. I want
to hide in the crevice of her sleep breath
& doze there, but the sun will expose me either way

the way childhood's books revealed
the secrets of sleight-of-hand.

Despite myself, I swallow when the swords are thrust through.

Tonight's moon wears the white robe of the initiate.
Slight blades of bats slice the air —

                              shadows on shadow

they move seemingly without effort although
I can almost hear the screech in their echo-locating throats.

Maybe in Syncopated Time

There are radio transmitters broadcasting deep
into space
          & probes launched back in the '70s
loaded with tracks from LPs so if aliens find them
they can play Beethoven or Miles Davis on their stereos

even if few people I know still have turntables.
Let's face it:
whatever intelligent life is out there may not groove
to Coltrane, may not snap whatever its equivalent of fingers
may be in syncopated time.
                        There were those nights
when, walking past Augie's, one tenor saxophone blown silken
would pull us in from the sidewalks,

swaddle us in melody — it was like being in love.
Afterward, we'd stroll the long blocks along Central Park
past the rounded hat of the Hayden Planetarium, &
the Museum of Natural History where I once saw

an exhibit of ancient brass instruments. In the SETI labs

the white lab coats scan for an anomaly —
the alien equivalent of the Song of Songs
or of Gillespie blowing Tunisia,

which must have sounded otherworldly at some point.

They hear nothing but static
& even the computers can't recognize a high C so high
it almost doesn't exist.

              Still, when I hear Miles
I can believe aliens have landed,
& when Coltrane chants *A love supreme. A love*
supreme, along with Jimmy Garrison's bass line
I can believe in a god
                    not of wrath or redemption
but of breath & tone.

Then it's gone
           leaving only hiss & static
like the sound between tracks on an old album,
the next song always just about to begin.

Contact Points

I understand little of even simple physics,
i.e., how batteries hold a charge or why
friction causes static electricity, though I do know
Ben Franklin studied the little blue sparks
caused by rubbing a stockinged foot, say,
along a rug, the way he studied the most domestic
gesture of a neighbor's daughter
& found it beautiful, the graceful bend of an arm
pouring water from a pitcher. Today
how you moved your neck just so
so your hair shifted (itself a source of kinetic energy)
made me recall the first time I touched the skin
under your shirt, that area
exposed when you stretch, blouse rising briefly,
that flesh just above the belt line …
What electrochemical reaction
shocked my finger so that even today
in the right light it still smolders. I try to picture
that place I touched beside your navel
how it flinched slightly, involuntarily,
rippled & relaxed. What science is it —
are there theorems, equations, proofs.
I admit we were kissing then, your hands
brushing my hair staticky. I admit
I haven't studied enough.

After Breakfast I Consider String Theory

I live by the river. — The Clash

Morgantown morning. In the distance
a train whistle from the west shore of the Monagahela River;
closer to home Joe Strummer's manic bird-like

uh-oh-oh! Oh-oh-oh! atop Paul Simonon's simple, steady bass

which shakes the window mist. Each day
the prior darkness lasts a bit longer,
                                        dawn hesitant
as a ninth grade boy's desire; the kids at the bus stop

discussing homework & gossip —

what does X equal? Did you hear who has a crush? —
awaiting the bright slices of bus headlights
carving the mist. When *London Calling* came out I was their age
& trying to understand the arithmetic of yearning

which I never mastered

though I inevitably learned to seem aloof, to master staring
                                                in the distance
as if at a spider web unfurled in the corner,
its engineer plump as a thumb, in slumber.
The web silvery with dew.

The bus is a Blue Bird bus,
October yellow with blue-black lettering for the school district
& a stylized bird in flight.

Do I alone see the irony in this?

The train carries loads of scrap & slag — hopper car
hopper car   hopper car — ten of these,

fifteen.

      If a train leaves Pittsburgh at 5:00 a.m. traveling south
and it passes Morgantown at 7:05,
X is how many miles per hour?
                        Its whistle is a mile away
so we hear it already a second after it occurred.

This is the problem of time, the problem of memory.

And so X is the phone number I was given once & lost.
And X is the number of light years across the known universe is.
And X is the street address of the house across from ours
with its furrowed awning & windows still dark.

But if X is nothing
more than the name of a girl in a class
that a boy writes over & over again like an incantation
in a marble notebook because he stutters when he feels it
                            on his tongue
& he is failing Math class for the first time ever,

what can be done? So it must be love,

the way the bound flies on the spider web must be hunger
& the Hubble photos of colored lights & gasses

must be the remnants of the universe's beginning,

the echo of the echo of the big bang.

Mist rising from the valleys & hollows in the mountain state
& the Eastern sky
slurring magenta from stark grey.

X is 7:08 a.m.
X is the mark on my hand to see a band in a bar that year
do a cover of "London Calling," & X
is the girl I spied there
diving from the stage
& how I dreamed her for months afterward

though I only saw her for a second, her body seemingly weightless

— hollow-boned —
so slight she was passed above the crowd.

The bus rumbles past my house & is gone,
the bus stop empty now but for the first leaves of autumn
kicking the air. X is the air in motion

& X is stillness. Outside

I step through a long strand of spider web

nearly invisible,
            but for the way it glistens like a thin rail
or, more precisely, like the high E-string of an electric guitar
                         in stage light:

little filament, little foundational cable.

A whole world disturbed momentarily.

From the telephone lines,
birds take off;
            moments later, other birds land.

Saint Sparrow

That afternoon among poplars & aspens I found it shrouded
among fallen leaves. Feathers like dandelion fluff
dispersed by the wind's breathy wish. Whatever killed
it had eaten & left these remains — toothpick bones,
skull like a hollow knuckle. Light
mottled green & shadowy all around, thickening
in the scent of decomposing foliage — a lushness
so deep in the nose it becomes a taste
like the supposed smell of a saint's incorruptible body.
I gathered that skeleton, held its small parts
& thus learned the secret of flight. Later,
as I reassembled it, & the desk lamp cast a patina
around each grey fragment, I thought of the Bible walk
behind the friary, its cast-off mannequins dressed
as prophets, beards long, clothes tattered now,
though at some point when the halls still reverberated
with vespers & matins, the monks must have tended
to these scenes, tailoring the outfits, repainting
each title (each sign shaped like Moses's two tablets),
stenciling in Old Testament chapter & verse, but not
any longer. The one Franciscan left, is he responsible
for their repair? Imagine him walking, infrequently,
that path, a roll of duct tape around his wrist
in case he needs to reattach a leg at the knee. For an hour
or two I worked like the boy I used to be, linking
bone to bone, puzzling it back together, until frustrated
I left it as it was — too many broken pieces,
too many missing shards. Still I kept some of vertebrae
in my pocket, which I shifted nightly so they were always
there — I could feel them like coins or keys against my thigh.
In the imperfect hours of my days, I'd finger them,
like a rosary of relics, knowing if I scattered them
on my night stand, they'd hardly be recognizable at all,
would resemble only a decade of lucky little stones.

Calabash

It grows in nests, in bound bunches
like bananas — each the size of the shrunken heads
we're told that Quequog sold. These green
fruit of beach blown trees aren't eaten but collected
by locals, cleaved & carved into
crafts: wall hangings, sculptures, masks.
I lift a calabash up, hold it in my hand
like a skull I want to listen to. I'll make
a mask of myself — shave a pair of glasses;
groove two dimples; shred palm fronds & glue them —
my wild recession; at the tip of its acorn shape,
a goatee. Not an amazing likeness,
but I'm there. I call it Gerard
and like this poem, it stares me submissive.
It seems to whisper or whistle
when I set it down. It knows too much.

While Listening to Burning Spear,
I Remember Sherry and her Father

He hung the machete in a place of honor
above the sofa; it was the tool, he told me,
that he had used in Jamaica to cut back brush —

his first job; his first earned dollars.

Each month he took it down, forbidding
tarnish, so he polished the blade like a warrior might
in the novels I read then.

It was a metaphor
for language, he said; something I already knew,
for I, too, had heard words cleave the space between Sherry & me
when we walked, hips rubbed together, into certain places

even in that city.
                    He never threatened me with it,

never suggested I not break his daughter's heart,
which I did not do

although when we split up I'm sure she wept
— just as I wept —
like an immigrant in a world that suddenly seemed

larger & smaller both.

He had wrapped the machete in newspaper & tape
& packed it in a suitcase
when he flew from Kingston to JFK.

For weeks afterward in a small Lower East Side flat
I imagine, he read those news stories
again & again. The Beatles or Jimi Hendrix on the alien radio.

He must've thought of the woman he'd left behind,
the way, today, I think of his daughter, how her heavy dreadlocks
swung so lightly,
when we'd dance nights at the Reggae Lounge,

his daughter not yet old enough
to talk, that August morning when he left;

He studied law those long days, & sometimes used that blade

to slice open a fresh mango or papaya bought on the street:
just a sweet, too-brief taste of the old world.

Perspective, St. Thomas, USVI

Now the wind turns the pages of my book
　　　　as if they were waves turning in on themselves,
a spray of words released, & so I look

again at what's happening. Little: a beach
　　　　holiday — my woman, an infrequent iguana, Ahab
pacing the Pequod's deck: the great whale unreach-

able always, like the sublime in the end, no matter
　　　　how many prayers, no matter the hours meditating
as dawn ignites the foamy edge of water,

no matter how many pleas of mercy
　　　　or anger. Call out the 10,000 names
of the divine, but still no reply, no pity,

no wish that gets fulfilled or even noted.
　　　　Once in a hotel pool near Philadelphia
I stared at a few visible stars, just floated

on my back hoping the water would carry me
　　　　all night, though, inevitably, I went inside
& wept, & nobody asked why, for nobody

had accompanied me. I offered that loneliness
　　　　up to god the way one might sacrifice fruit.
That's the closest I've been to holiness

my night like a cloister. Since then I've shrunk
　　　　away from the sacred, but all that miserable year
I played ascetic, fancied myself some secular monk.

So how did I wind up here beside the Atlantic
        while she's in the water or in our room or tanning
beside me as I read *Moby Dick* — ?

I can't say. In the wind, palm fronds
        on their branches creak & sigh, waves froth,
a green iguana watches me intently, then it's gone.

Walking Meditation, Early A.M.

> *Question six: … Why does Buddhism encourage entering*
> *realization through meditation only in sitting?*
> *Answer: The Ancestor praises it, saying, "Zazen itself is the*
> *dharma gate of ease and delight." So shouldn't we infer that it's*
> *because [sitting] is the most stable and peaceful of the four postures.*

Walk to the end of the block

                  or the end of the continent &

still no change, though the sand is wet with retreating tide.

Old men fish in the surf
while others remain

                strolling the boardwalk of dreams.

Sea gull sound

           & wave sound become one.

The tenor of a distant prop plane harmonizes.
It pulls a sign I can't quite read.

Geology says farther west is Kamchatka, Serbia, Ireland eventually …
Physics says if you can't see it, it may no longer exist.
Zen master says either way it doesn't change how you breathe.

I've lived my life with such conflict:

the shells I pick up are evidence of mollusks; the deep imprint of bodies
& the empty sail of a condom wrapper
proof of desire

               that only time & wind can erase.

Who can sit on a day like this?

All morning I walk the beach like I've walked Avenue B,

trying to be aware of my own awareness.

There are no junkies here. No bodegas. No corners.
No men unfold mini flea markets across blankets.

Once on the way from Fourteenth St. to Houston,
I bought a copy of *Hot Rocks* for fifty cents
after sorting through records in a shopping cart.

On my turntable later,
                    the album hissed & sputtered
Mick's voice skipping: *I can't _____ no satisfaction.*

I sat for ten minutes
                    trying to make those lyrics my mantra.

When I went back to Avenue B, the man had been replaced
by a regiment of pigeons.
Who can say now if it really happened?

Geology says we record time —
                    look at the fossil record.
Physics says time is interdimensional —
                                        but warps with gravity.
Zen master asks if I'm the same person now I was then.

I could sit here breathing all day, here
                                    where a couple fucked
last night, unable or unwilling to wait,
but would whatever answer I came up with be acceptable?

The fishermen cast & wait. Cast again.

Buoy bells call six times.
The wind shifts like an uncomfortable sleeper,
brings with it a whiff of coffee & maple syrup.

I want to walk into enlightenment

as if it were a shop to enter.

From a Room Overlooking the Beach

St. Thomas, USVI

All over the island the blossoms of flamboyants
— blatantly red —
like the robes of tiny Tibetan monks.
At sunset the trade winds shake their bodies
and you can almost hear their mantras

then silence —

What of the iguana?
What of the anole — its anomalous color
changing from brown to green as it worries
from the path into shrubs?

Such transformation evidence of transcendence.

Later I can hear the sparks
of a pan drum being hammered.
                              Each note a star
palpable & brilliant; they ascend from the beach

up the seventy steps meant to ease
this mountain topography & keep rising

to bless the blue glow of televisions burning in distant windows;
to bless even briefly the bruised silences.

Poem Found Among Scraps
in a Lower East Side Gutter

Say: tymbales. Feel the tymbales' light
like coffee percolating on your tongue. Its rhythm —
countless woodpeckers working

a hollow trunk, but with a beat,
an urgent need to dance. Thus love is in the tymbales
as Tito Puente always claimed. Last night

in the goldenrod glaze of First Avenue lights, I watched
a vagrant with headphones hiding
his ears, its long unplugged cord swaying

below his waist as he pumped his arms to
whatever melody he listened to, a pair of drumsticks —
one in each fist. When Tito Puente died,

mourners sent hundreds of carnations to his hospital room
& some DJs played his songs
24 hours straight. Few people listened, though

it's easy to imagine some lovers tuned in,
fucking with each song until, at the moment
when both of them seem to levitate,

they called each other's name & called to god &

so attested to the divinity of that moment. Outside
traffic passed with its rush hour lethargy,
taxi horns cacophonous, their extended notes bending

like muted trumpets, like night itself. In the rain
on the roof: tymbales

& in the kiss of the woman I love, tymbales &

in the sound of my son running downstairs,
tymbales; outside that homeless guy
still dances, slower now, in the intersection

his hand still clutching those drumsticks. Whatever beat
he hears, he moves as if through water, but gracefully —
even the drivers who pass him hesitantly turn

their heads for one last look. Later,
recounting the story from a living room couch,
some will swear they recognized him —

a high school chum, perhaps,
or one cousin's distant gaze
as in a family photo from when we were children.

The Sacrosanct

In Manhattan again, in the midst of midtown businessmen
& women with briefcases & designer sunglasses
I stop at D'agostino's where I buy two apples,
two blood oranges & two apricots. I am not
hungry. There's the R train downtown
to Canal Street, Chinatown's sulfurous tip.
I walk East & South in blocks
to find this place I've been many times
before; as always I bow to the Buddha
& to the old woman who sweeps the floor
& to the monk's creased bald head.
He is a walking wick, aglow, in his silence.
I place two apricots, two oranges &
an apple before the statue. There's enough fruit here
already — grapefruits bigger than my fists, mangos,
bananas. & what of my other apple?
I gave it to the rag man bound for Brooklyn.
He eyed the fruit suspiciously, holding it
up to the artificial light for sixty long seconds
till finally he bit into it with a spray of sweet juices
that christened his chin, golden in that yellow glow.
Mmm delicious, he said, *delicious* like a chorus;
rocking southbound, seventy feet beneath those streets.

Soursop & Oranges

We weren't surprised exactly
(our faces still puckered from the soursop we'd plucked)
by wild donkey — three of them —

grazing like store detectives. All I could recall:
the oranges I picked illegally
that time in Florida — how I parted their thick skins

with my thumbs until my hands glistened
& the juicy citrus blossomed into sections
like young desire — there was a strange girl;

we were thirteen or fourteen & we were
hungry in ways we didn't
yet comprehend. How could I explain?

I couldn't. Still can't, not to the donkey anyway.
But the fruit was delicious & cool
on the tongue like a first kiss.

Go Hawaiian

In eighth grade, Jill Frangos & I sang
the Hawaiian Punch theme song like Donny & Marie; not like them
we kissed in the coat closet
     or behind the church
where we confessed our sins & tried to make each other giggle

before Eucharist. In eighth grade we made promises to each other
we didn't know
     we couldn't keep. In eighth grade

Jill Frangos shot twenty-four foul shots in a row
while I hit two (my third missing hoop & backboard
completely). She didn't care:

her voice like candy thrown at a parade.

In eighth grade I knew nothing
& still scored perfectly on algebra exams, history exams
spelling exams & so earned a spot in the back corner
right beside Jill Frangos. There we sang & made fun

& invited each other over
for Friday night fish dinners with spaghetti.

Her mother once chaperoned us
at the roller rink: we skated the oval countless times
our fingers interlocked,
     counter-clockwise
with the other skaters, as if we were all trying
to keep it eighth grade forever:
     already my voice faltered

when we sang Hawaiian Punch, already my facial hair
darkened. When Jill Frangos fell that day

she pulled me down
beside her for a minute as long as eighth grade

while our laughter diffused
in the scattered dimes of a disco ball's light,
& neither of us wanted to get back up.

A Kind of Holiness

Then a shoplifter ran across the street
followed by a cashier. Then a choir of brakes emphasized
by the percussion of a body contacting a car fender.
Then sobbing.
    And, eventually, sirens.

We were there — a crowd of us — & among us may have been
the thief who had slipped back to see what had happened,
some bauble — how little was it worth? — in his pocket
that he fingered.
    Then police officers dispersed the crowd

ensuring us there was nothing to see, which wasn't exactly true.

Years passed,
rain washed whatever blood had been spilled down the gutters,
water cascading toward the sewer grates. I was lonely then —

I kept my head downcast no matter what the weather
& whatever I witnessed I never snitched.

This, I believed, was a kind of holiness,

though that night after I undressed for bed I prayed
for the woman & the driver & the thief who worked

in the noble tradition of those who hung beside Jesus,

prayed on my knees the way that nuns had taught,
prayed for myself, too, & for the last time …

For the last time, that is, till tonight
when I thought of you & thought of my loneliness, then heard

sirens cresting Little Savage Mountain
& knew I had this one opportunity to make something — even

if I won't say what — make something right again.

Counting Past 100

Fallen leaves on the grounds of the Capuchin Monastery
& on the lawns of all my neighbors —

the first day after
                        the first autumnal rain.
So now raking & the hornet hum of leaf blowers
distantly, & behind that, the smell of damp October smoldering.

Years ago I taught Alex to count using the leaves
smattered in the yard, which means, really, I taught him futility.

Today I've counted past 100,
not the fallen, but my sins. Whatever pleasure

I took from them is gone, only their husks remain
almost festering   almost pretty

like the laughter of those nuns I once saw,
their habits blustery in the blustering wind
as they played putt-putt golf,
                                    particularly after one swore
a *Goddamn!* upon missing par.

I've given up the confessional & the rake both
& who's noticed? October

in its dark coat with its silver courier bag slung low,
walks on to make the switch at the Feast of Saints —
such a troubled rogues gallery, that bunch.

The nuns taught me the familiar prayers I threw away;
the friars taught me humility & not to masturbate.
Nothing practical.

Nearly 40, I know nothing
                                about being an adult
despite all evidence to the contrary.
When my son comes to me for advice or money I shrug
though I can at least unfold the comfort of bills —

just another bribe
                        to conceal my shortcomings. Therefore,
I tally up the cardinal & venial both on my adding machine
& will have to include this fib on the list,

but first I'd like to walk beside October,
walk with it into that leaf smoke & whatever's beyond.

Poem Found in the Graffiti on a Freight Train's Cars

Across the Monongahela a freight train pushes southward, hauling
a long load of empty hopper cars. So slowly,
I watch for awhile, light glinting off their painted bodies.

They go down track up into the mountains to be filled with coal
& later I'll hear a heavier train, northbound
for steel mills & power plants.
                                        Coal smoke omen-black.
Molten ore white-orange
so workmen look distantly, despite protective visors,

their faces tanned, fissured with sweat canals. They pour steel
for rails & car parts, for girders & bolts.

The first transcontinental railroad worked its way like a needle
followed by a thick thread of telegraph cable across the plains;
operators working Morse code for Western Union

sending boys with messages to banks & newspapers
& to ministers in their white clapboard churches, working on sermons,
the King James version at hand when news came to prepare a funeral.

Did anyone ever send a poem by telegraph —
                                        & to whom? Imagine
Whitman converted to clicking dots & dashes:
Have you reckoned a thousand acres much? Have you reckoned
                                        the earth much? Stop.

Have you practiced so long to learn to read? Stop.

Imagine the shock of those men at their desks
interpreting each line. Their normal boredom dusty in station offices,
in towns across America — their casual conversations

with conductors & engineers. I think of Sam on that long train
⠀⠀⠀⠀⠀⠀⠀⠀⠀⠀⠀⠀⠀⠀⠀⠀⠀⠀⠀⠀⠀⠀to Portland, 1988;
what does she look for, head pressed against the seat back? —
swaying fields of crops or occasional shacks, miles of highway parallel.

Sun on it all & on the train's silver & glass body,
so it's almost as if she travels in light itself.
⠀⠀⠀⠀⠀⠀⠀⠀⠀⠀⠀⠀⠀⠀⠀⠀⠀⠀⠀⠀⠀⠀Then silence for 17 years.

This morning I breathed the waking birdsong the way I used to
meditate walking the tracks behind my Roscommon house.

⠀Taking breaths with each cross tie,
⠀⠀⠀⠀⠀⠀⠀⠀⠀⠀⠀⠀⠀⠀⠀⠀⠀⠀or else Alex & I would walk
between the rails.
He was four then & already I was preparing for his departure.

Sometimes he'd hear a low whistle nearing
& come from his room, sleep trailing, calling *Train! Train!*
He'd run outside, waving to the engineers in those
diesel engines the color of sky, & many would wave back

or pull the whistle again as if to say: *Hello!*
⠀⠀⠀⠀⠀⠀⠀⠀⠀⠀⠀⠀⠀⠀⠀⠀⠀⠀As if to say: *Come follow.*
As if to say: *The Lord advances and yet advances:*
Always the shadow in front … .

The Silence That Follows

It's early summer in Grayling, & death has no business here
despite my neighbor celebrating his 93rd June.
Black flies convene above

                    the ruffled surface of the AuSable
while adolescents dream of canoeing toward Wakely Bridge
with dates or their fathers. On street corners

the stands are up, some selling cherry bombs & rockets,
some selling Old Mission cherries. I knew a young woman,
yes, years ago, who could twist

                    cherry stems into knots
with her tongue, & what young man wouldn't love that?
All I could do was spit the pits of those tart fruits

& never far enough to win a ribbon at Cherry Fest.
All I could do was tell her *I love you*, but
there was no ribbon for that, either.

                    Still, I'll stop my car
along the shoulder of West 72, buy a pound of cherries
& admire their merlot bodies, their skin

taut & rounded. I could be in love all over again
with the scent of fresh cherries. When it ended
there was nothing our tongues could do,

                    no words we might tie
together to make anything all right. Her name translates
into *I love* or *I like*. I lived three blocks from Mercy Hospital then

though there was no mercy to be had that long August
in the empty cardboard of our house. I sat & listened
to ambulances rushing in.

                    The siren howled like a lonely man
or like a lonely woman. It's early summer in Grayling,

& I have three dollars worth of cherries, & I never did learn

how she did that trick with her tongue & the stem,
though I used to finger those knots like a Persian
reading a rug. Translation's
                            such a subjective art. I'd say
her name twice in a row — *I like   I like* —
& now I've stopped saying it at all, & stopped even

thinking of her. Tonight I'll eat Michigan cherries from brown paper
& from my porch watch an ambulance hurry with its charges.
Behind it, a car full of prayers.
                            In the silence that follows
I might hear the river only a block away:
a quick splashing of something crossing over to the near shore.

Manchineel

Our tour guide mentions the manchineel
— the death apples — on St. John,
tells us not to run for protection
beneath those trees: their acid sap burns holes

in clothes, blisters the flesh. Around us
nature in carnivale: flashy hibiscus,
the oleander & flamboyant call across resort courtyards.
Yes it's like paradise, he assures,

his voice a trade wind. Later, we'll listen to calypso;
after that, to anoles changing their colors
like lives. We'll cut a mango
into delicious sunlight slivers,

but first this juggler at Mongoose Bay
with three of those fruits in the air,
his fingers scalded & scarred,
which he's more than willing to display,

then bow — all for tourist tips. Impressed
we leave our dollars while our guide continues:
What fruit was it in Eden? That's simple.
He flashes one tooth. *Was death apple. Death apple.*

Thinking of the Franciscan Abbey
after Reading James Wright

*Due to declines in their orders, many monasteries now have only
one friar — a caretaker monk — remaining in their buildings.*

In the monastery, the last monk has given up
his vow of silence.
He speaks quietly to each accusatory wind
coming through the gaps in masonry.
What man of faith wouldn't think
such drafts were the Holy Spirit?
With all his brothers gone or gone on,
who is left to offend?
He still wakes at five to pray in the chapel
— end-of-summer light through stained glass:
dusty shafts of green, goldenrod, royal blue
& the haloes of all those saints fiery.
An echo of his steps through the corridors
makes him think sometimes that he isn't
alone. Who hasn't felt this way before?
What sort of god would come as a thief
at night, he thinks, & not as a brother
arms open for embrace?

After Reading Rexroth I Step Outside

Low moon tonight & nearly full.
See how it illuminates the alien bodies of mushrooms
colonizing the weedy lawn. They're a surprise after six weeks
of near drought, delivered, no doubt,

                              by the drizzle that followed —

their fibrous necks lifting up their heads so they seem to look
in wonder. There was that time

I went morel hunting with a woman I thought I loved;
we carried two plastic grocery bags
& a blanket & lunch.
                       We spent our morning searching
around the bases of birch & pine,
& by the area, also, where fire had created a richness of soil.

I had thought maybe we'd find some mushrooms, eat lunch,
& then make love on that blanket,
the smell of moist nature — of decay & growth —
surrounding us
                 & thus that ground would be consecrated.

But we were confounded
to find, at first, the bones of what we believed to be
a large animal, some ribs & vertebrae,

&, excited by our discovery, we dug around till we found
the long femur of what was most likely a young child,
a handful of metatarcels.
                          How she drew in her breath
— a slight, high-pitched whistle.

The flesh, of course, was gone — who knows how long
the body had rotted in the rotten earth.
The police arrived inevitably; inevitably,

we had to retrace our steps back to that place
a mile from a state highway
                              where she had laid the blanket
above the remains & held it firm with rocks
as if such a gesture could make a difference.

All that first night she wept & shivered, &
there was no comforting her,
                              for who could sleep

with milky light filling our bare windows in that way.

Train Whistle Far from Town, Approaching

Dawn on the neck of a broken bottle
there on the train tracks through the woods

so that, lit up this way, deep green &
brilliant, the shards have an almost alien
beauty as if they've been dyed in light.

If such days have a flavor, would they taste
of vanilla or honeysuckle or Chardonnay?

Would they taste of her shampoo & sweat?
More bitter? All night I'd battled nostalgia
while the wind along the rails sounded

like a harmonica, sudden blues
that hinted of Chicago. There's been too much

loss for me to walk laughing into first light,
so I'll just sit, here
in the living room & wait for another train

to rattle these walls. Somewhere
the Gatsbys of this world are hosting

their grand parties. Still, the boxcars carry echoes
of their laughter & carry the good hoboes, too,
who have forsaken jobs cashiering gas stations,

& heartache, & kitchen floors that need
to be scrubbed, traded them for metronomic

rail wheels. Such times, when the train slows
as it curves through town, I try to imagine

them carousing while they warm their hands

in the glow of green glass, & beneath that joy
the undeniable silence

that marks despair. In spite of myself
I want to call to them
believing, finally, I have found my people.

January 1, 2008

First squirrel of the year walks westward on its wire
while the trees shudder
then steady. In the middle of my sleep

sirens woke me & then were gone.

Now morning unpacks its suitcase of sunlight
& the brilliant blue of promise mixes with regret.

This is how the wind moves us all & pushes
the moral of our story further into obscurity.

Having gotten its invitation, a storm front will visit
later, heading east as if to meet the day.

Walking the Neighborhood
the Morning after a Snow Storm

A salt truck growls like the neighbor's dog.
The north wind shakes my right hand, then, enraged,
slaps my face with its left. Grey light vivid
on the dunes of snow. Metal taste of cold surrounds me.
Last night the storm crackled, broken glass
falling; the sleet stung scattershot. Finally morning,
the front faltering & dragging its heavy scent with it,
a radio voice poked me awake —
the way it said *icy conditions* was the way Beth Staub
might have said it in Kalamazoo,
except she never used that phrase, not once in the year
we tossed each other smiles.
There haven't been any of the usual cats out these days,
clawing through garbage bags & spraying
their graffiti of piss. They've been dissed by the meteorologist.
And since the cats are gone,
the mailman will bring three bills today. How lucky!
You can't burn the fur off a squirrel,
at least not on a day such as this:
the winter pennies of regret rattling in my cupped hands
& silence following in the wake of that truck
like an echo. But I can walk above the drifts without
falling through & can recall every song lyric
by the Rolling Stones. Gerard's no saint,
though he knows both Catechism & cataclysm,
so he'll sing these songs in his best Mick Jagger
all evening & into tomorrow
& beyond if need be, beginning with "Jumping Jack Flash."
The delinquent wind won't care,
won't applaud but won't howl louder to drown me out either.
I couldn't be any happier in this sadness.
Bravo! Bravisimo! The morning whistles

toward afternoon while the warmth of the house
extends a finger my way, seductive;
from under the doorway I can hear Keith Richards
kicking off "She's so Cold"
as the DJ finishes up the weather atop its opening riffs.

Storm Front, Moving East

Now rain fumbles the keyboard of a piano
some neighbors pulled to the curb; so many keystrokes

& still no sound, the way silence emanated last night

when I drove past as a young boy stood before it,
hands arced, fingers running imaginary sprints,

each gesture hyperbolized, cartoonish
as if he were playing some too-much-Bugs-Bunny blues,
some my-parents-never-let-me-play-

this blues: all of it mute
                              as deepening grey clouds arrived & stayed.

I pull the shade, allow it to snap upward, & look out
past the back yard, over the closed neighborhoods,
trash bags piled before each home,

sometimes a box or broken appliance

& local cats that scratch through plastic
to drag a chicken carcass onto the sidewalk. Beyond all this

the fall's full moon sneaking through.
It was Aristotle who believed children
ought to be taught music — such bird-like leisure — ,

& who hasn't needed a song when loneliness comes,
selling its magazine subscriptions.

                              Not this morning though,
which is briefly jarred by a garbage truck turning

followed by the whine of air brakes &
growl of hydraulics crushing waste. I expect soon

to hear cracking mahogany, the metallic grind of cables
right before they snap.
                    Rather, from beneath the truck's fumey rumble

bass notes
& then a moment of jump blues, the driver jamming
a little Jelly Roll —
                    the melody
out of tune, warped, wavering, some notes completely
absent when those hammers strike nothing, but still

it comes darting from the sidewalk, each note like a bottle rocket
toward the waning bank of nimbostratus,
which already hefts its load toward Baltimore & D.C.

The Hawk and Its Shadow Fly the Same Pattern

To the west, mountains; to the west,
sunset the color of a blood orange, its juice spreading
behind wisps of nimbus. So much of the world
momentarily in silhouette. Not myself, sadly —

I'm reminded by how easily the world can be split:
tricks of light. Sensei still teaches
non-duality, & I still nod my head
except when I don't — & doesn't that just prove him right?

Sometimes I can't tell enlightenment from smugness,
so maybe, just maybe, they're the same thing. Backlit
this way these hawks could be angels
— wings stretched at such precise angles, the way

they glide, seemingly without effort.
I've quartered a blood orange & lifted one piece
to my mouth, bit its pulpy flesh &
sucked such sweetness dry. I might've shared

surely, but those other three sections were just as
tasty — I'm sorry Dr. Williams. I'm sorry,
mi amor. There are some things I won't share,
some moments so startling they can only be

described not in the language of hawks nor in
the language of the wind that holds such hawks
aloft, but in the sublime geometry, proven
by the concave arc in the underside of their wings.

Elegy for my 34th Year

Summer dusk. Despite its bellyful of recent rain, the Monongahela
                                          murmurs northward
&, even murmuring, it has a slight drawl
echoing the mountain towns along its banks where former union men

complain about mine shut downs & mill closures
while old women stand among weedy yards, tsking their tongues.

Their patience is a form of fidelity.
                              From the river's Westover shore,

two streetlamps unfurl halogen ribbons along the surface,
one a band of white   one a band of saffron,
both rippled with shadow, & between them
                              darkness. Between them

the river murky with coal run off & deeper than it's been in years.

There's no baptism in such water,
                              nor in the light reflected on it.
No forgiveness. Earlier,

as I walked this former railroad track, a man called out, *Pilgrim,*
where are you heading? The answer was nowhere
                              although that didn't seem right,

so I stayed silent.
So, I let the Monongahela whisper its vespers.
So, I stopped on this bridge parallel to the river & watched insects
fly haphazard patterns around a trail light,
                              some of them softly trilling.

A mathematician friend might write the equation of such flight
& call it god; I can even see her
at a whiteboard with red & black markers:

variables & numbers graffitied in the wake of her hand.
Her faith in these formulae, scrawled as they are
in the rhythm of her penmanship, a type of religion

like my belief in morning coffee,
like my belief in the rain that has resumed:
slight drizzle falling in its own logical pattern,

                              water level rising exponentially

here, near the Morgantown bank of this river
& in the mountains, distant & shrouded by evening, which I know

                                                    are there,

& in the shafts of interspersed light
& in the rings each drop makes: rippling circles,

like shimmery halos in those paintings of the prophets.

Pineapple

So much like the punk girls
I desired then — green spiked hair

& the tough exterior, dangerous
to touch: a studded leather jacket

zipped tight. But the fruit
inside — golden light

wildly unexpected until eaten,
doled out in pieces & in rings,

the juice sticky on my chin
so sweet & fresh, so acidic.

Perfidia

Sunday begins with the Ventures,
with that trebly lead guitar, tremoloed just right —
their sound a perfect trinity

of blues, rock-&-roll, & Hawaiian.
That's how surf was born,
                    the songs like waves.

The neighborhood church, like a fire siren,
calls the faithful to ten o'clock services.
An excited flurry of bells.
                    On the first spring morning
in this, the 2009th year of our Lord,
in another 1,000,000 dollar weekend I can't afford,

I'll excuse myself, again, from mass
& from the prayers I've never forgotten,
& from the hymns I sang through childhood —

Let there be peace on earth,
& let it begin with me ...
                    Yeah sure, the guitars counter.
Nokie Edwars playing lead again, all vibrato & reverb,
that familiar lick: *Walk, don't run.*

One Bird Feeder Feeds at Least Four Dozen Birds

Just before dawn they arise —
$\qquad\qquad$ each with its own music.

On the morning news an almost well-dressed anchor
gives the gruesome details of a local homicide — a forty-year old

man found by a neighbor,
the body's arms duct-taped behind its back,
$\qquad\qquad\qquad$ eyes still open, wide

as if stunned by some brilliance. The newscaster keeps smiling.
Outside: gray light inches slightly closer to full day:

time & light helixed together
so that — however it's going to happen — I'm already minutes closer

to my own death. So are you. Not much
we can do about it, either,
$\qquad\qquad$ though I keep promising I'll change my life.

The paper says the murdered man may have walked in on a robbery;
the neighbor had seen the door
$\qquad\qquad\qquad$ unlatched early the next day
& had investigated. The police have a toll-free number

for information. How often do I have to be reminded

it's not what we want that leads to suffering,
but wanting itself. In America,
even Zen teachings have been reduced to t-shirts

although some people believe the fat birds near the feeders
just may be reincarnated

Bodhisattva. They've no anxiety but in the present tense.
No pleasure either

        except in song.

There's no better moment than now, they might well sing.
Or else: *Thank you! Fuck you! Thank you!*

See: I've learned little & little's changed:

I could walk out there with seed or suet & they'd still
flee to the lowest limbs, whistling & clicking

                            as if filled
with some good news they'd rather not share.

Treatise on the Possibility of a God of Love

Open husks of chestnuts
                    by the grounds of St. Michael's,
each hollow space like a mouth agape,

like the bed after she said she was gone for good,
like the tomb of Jesus
                    that third day.
The disciples either weeping or enraged.

I had always thought the story could be an allegory
for romance —
                    all that loss & redemption,
that reliance on faith — a notion

which the Christian Brothers in their bleak prayers
worked to correct.
                    Maybe they were right.

All day I've missed her
& still church bells every fifteen minutes

& the postman with his sack full of bills & circulars.

He's singing a song I don't recognize,
but it might as well go: *I'm happy. So happy!*

with the squirrels. There are times when I've felt so much awe
with the good things of this world that I've stood
slack jawed & earnest
                    hoping to carry that sensation
like a love letter to be posted.

Not today,
although the leaves do crunch underfoot,
a surprisingly satisfying sound.

Fire Engine, Early Morning

Listen: there's something beautiful
in a fire engine's wail past midnight,
the way my mother has been prettiest
in her anguish, eyes red-rimmed. See
the summoned heads stretched from
fourth floor windows, turned eastward.
Is that aura in the distance flames
or ordinary metropolitan glare?
Which way does the wind come from
perfumed with smoke? Once
I slept through a small blaze in the living room
of an upstairs apartment,
slept through clarions outside my window
& the lieutenant's heavy fist against my door.
These nights I sleep less & thus read about Odysseus
lashed to the mast just so
he could listen to those beautiful,
dangerous arias — how he must've wept
at his bindings; imagine Troy smoldering.
What does it say that I don't consider Dresden,
or Nagasaki, or the towers
that Tuesday morning, five days after
a surgeon removed my mother's left breast
& so she wasn't in the wave of that debris.
What does it say that, instead,
I think of a jet at the county airport
circling, dumping fuel before descending,
emergency vehicles lined up by the tarmac —
just in case. It came down safely
in the end, & the civilian air patrol members cheered
though there were some on the ground, I thought,
who turned away to hide their disappointment.

Upper East Side, Winter 2002

I finally step back into that February Friday,
the hospitals doors whooshing gently closed behind me.
The wind calls out.
York Avenue stretches dark

as the sutures sealing my mother's neck.
So I walk south, amazed at the people in restaurant windows,

some with their heads back,
                              mouths wide in laughter

which means the City is recovering, though still
on a light post, faded & frayed posters: the photographs;
Have you seen?; the phone numbers.

I hold hands with no one but the evening
& remember how, as a child, I had to run beside my mother
just to keep up with her. She navigated the streets in a manner

I never thought I'd know — aware of each cross street & where
to find what we needed.

                    Wrong again, it seems.
In the antiseptic hallway her oncologist reassured us —

my mother more worried about this new scar
than her absent breast. Yes, there had been a different surgeon
only a few months before.

                    I have to return to her apartment.
I have to curse.
I have to
count, like Rosary beads, all the churches & synagogues I pass

because who among us can escape our need for hope?
On a few corners, still, novena candles melt
beside badges & obituaries.

It's a different urge that leads me, twenty blocks later,
into a pizzeria where I wait at the counter

till the slice comes from the oven, haloed with steaming grease.
Then I join the others there,
                          the lonely men, each at his own table,
& the young mother who strokes down her son's cowlick
before they get up to leave.

Cold Sun Over Queens

Walking up from a warm subway, my legs shaky
I stop for coffee & a donut from a street cart
to comfort myself, then continue east.

A block farther I pour that coffee
into the gutter, watch its weak bitterness steam.
I waste
          so I shall want again. In this way

I'm so American, & in this way, too, I'm disappointed
by a cathedral's bolted doors, frost
on its stained glass. Such avoidance.

is what I know: Memorial Sloane Kettering
where my mother lay; a Korean woman
in the other bed complaining bitterly & in Korean

to a tired daughter who sleeps on a cot
nearby. IV bags slowly deflating.
Nurses talking the language of nurses

& pharmaceuticals. For the last two days
I've thought this place — the head & neck ward —
the saddest place, until this morning,

when volunteers roll two kids my son's age
into the elevator, their heads tufted —
thin hair feathery; their skin translucent

so I can see the artery near the skull's crest
pulse regularly. When I exit on the 8th floor
I crash into an orderly who lands on her ass.

She opens her mouth to let loose
100 dark birds of laughter among the gurneys
& wheelchairs, so that even walking patients

one hand pushing an IV stand, one hand
on a loved one's arm, even they turn. Smile.
How can we think to laugh, right now?

In my mother's room I avoid the garish grin
black thread makes from under her right ear,
down her neck,
                                    then across her throat

where the surgeon had done his routine job:
removing another thyroid from another patient.
We small talk, watch midday television

& maybe go up to the top floor to make art
or listen to a different patient's daughter play
Mozart on the Steinway, each note a tear

I refuse. Twelve hours a day I stay
& feel guilty for leaving & for wanting to leave,
& for wanting to break my mother out

as if she were held hostage. This last Saturday,
as I exit again into darkness, I feel five
briefly, standing by a different hospital

alongside my mother with the local 1199, on strike —
the men with lab coats & cigarettes, picket signs
by their side. My hand sweaty in hers

as it was when I kissed her goodnight — how much
unsaid? So I ask one nurse for a smoke
my mother would disapprove of;

the Bic's flame like a taper. Neither of us
notes the irony of smoking here,
& because I hadn't had a cigarette in years

I cough & know, walking west with it,
that I'll waste it *too*, but before flicking it away,
I inhale a few more times, that illicit warmth

filling my chest, the small round tip glowing
like a distant star, the night cold, & the moon,
the moon has turned its dark back to all of us.

Alphabet City

Avenues A through D, Lower East Side, NYC

After the ambulances left but
before the sun finally rose above Avenue
C, I walked toward Tompkins Square Park where the heroin-
dependent rockers slept, addled on benches, while
ex-punks huddled in their leather jackets
for the morning was still damp. One of them called out,

Gerry? What was I to do when I saw her, recognized
her hesitant familiar eyes. How could I have
imagined things would turn out this way when I'd call out *her* name —
Joanna — those sleepless nights of high school &
kept a photo of her deep into college.
Longing has such a sense of history.

Morning was approaching in its colorful coat.
Not once those months of kissing her, had I wakened beside her, but
oh — I'd wanted to. She was thinner & glanced away when I nodded;
pigeons surrounded her bench but would take off
quickly with the first sudden movement or when the next squad car
revealed itself in flashers & sirens.

So what did I do? What could I do?
The three five dollar bills folded in my pocket, what
use were they to me? I gave them to her, she who'd once been
                                        beautiful. How
victorious I'd felt that first time I kissed her.

We didn't look at each other, nor did we look askance. I thought
                                        of the little

xiphoid syringes she might load with that money. This was my sin.

Two

young black kids with dreadlocks walked by singing
Zion! Take me back to Zion! & I knew I'd never be saved.

Perspective: New York City

On Avenue B, a homeless guy asks our names, says
God bless you & *Thank you* for each donation
be it dime or dollar. Used to be a dime
could buy a phone call, a dollar could book you a ride
through four boroughs on the trains. New York
1985, summer heat so intense I swear dimes melted
into asphalt by the basketball parks where homeboys
played one-on-ones for a dime a basket.
Days so windless nothing moved the nets;

yes there were nets: that year New York sent crews
to net each hoop, five-and-dime store nets
that would, for the most part, be gone by summer's end.
The kids argued who was better, the Knicks or Nets,
the Yanks or Mets. In some ways then New York
hasn't changed, & we stand against the steel net of a hurricane fence
& watch the kids net basketballs, the rhythmic dribble
like subway chatter, though now the stakes are higher —
dollar a bucket. We're watching these two guys play,
caches of dollars switching pockets after each game.
Five net difference, five dollars.
Though they seem even to me, I'm sure they can say
who's had a net gain, a net loss
for the evening. When it's over they high five &

disperse into New York evening. New York is the cologne
I want to wear. New York's the empty space
in the grooves of my fingertips, New York was
the night school where I learned to net hook shots & pitch
dimes & ride the subways from Lower East Side streets to Queens
where you were spending dollars on girls named Lanette or Beth,
their eyes big as dimes, burnished like dimes.
Each dollar a love poem, each dollar

a votive candle in the churches we didn't attend,
each dollar a promise. George Washington,
who snared the Red Coats, was inaugurated in New York, downtown
Wall Street, two blocks from where I once made five dollars an hour

& off Avenue B someone has spray painted a mural of Washington,
Martin Luther King & Gandhi. *Only in New York*, you say
& say it again when two guys in hair nets & subway uniforms
appear at the court, a dime bag & cigarettes set down
as they pick up their ball. They smell like sandwich meat
& patchouli. They smell like dollar bills & subway platforms,
like spilled beer, like hands that have held too many dimes.
When they look up & see us leaning against the fence,
they'll invite us to play some two-on-two.
What will we say? How good's our give-and-go?
The moon small as a half-dollar so it's hard to believe
men ever leapt on its surface & stared down
at the earth, trying to make out the lights of New York.

Mango

Delicious slivers of mango
cut like long tongues — so it's as if we eat
our passion, this longing

sticky like the afterglow of sex,
our skin the reddish mottle of mango skin.
So often I've eaten these alone,

bought at some Upper West Side bodega
& sliced open with a pocket knife.
I'd sit in Riverside Park, sunset

orange in the Hudson below:
sunset orange with a knife blade in it,
bleeding orange in my hands.

Phenomenology of the Vanishing Horizon

Tortola, B.V.I.

Because a life is laden with departures,
I stopped at the airstrip to watch another 737 approach,
twin lights barely aglow in Carribean heat,
its metallic torso almost graceful
                              — how many tons in the air?

Lowering steadily offshore,
                              its jets issued a flotilla of spray
which diffracted the light
& then it was done

but for the engines' distracted roar, the rush of wind I knew
was the wing flaps turning upward.

Even from that distance, I could feel moisture.

From certain points here you look east at nothing but sea & sky,

the problems of latitude & longitude. To the west

the humped back of islands
dropped like a child's toys, some so close
you can see resplendent flowering trees: magenta, orange, violet blurs.

Beaches shouldering surf. Yes,
there are always boats, white bodies bobbing on their lines with the tides.

A young shark swims in the shallows. Truly,
it's beautiful: the length of my arm
from fingertips to elbow, its body a mix of glimmer
& shade. It follows the shore

sputters in a wave's waning moment
then shimmies away

                     toward deeper water. In the shadow
play of breakers,
I lose sight of it.

What's a wave but an ever-changing curve,
a mathematical anomaly?

Because these islands are isolated
like aesthetes in their chambers, praying, many are named for

                                            saints;

like churches I attended years ago,

smell of incense rubbed into pews. I learned
to genuflect & mark a cross
on four points of the body — both shoulders, forehead, chest: places
where sin may lie.

Tonight, slight spray of sea as I walk the shoreline:
the Southern Cross like four moments of holy water.

Again wave sound lulls us to sleep
& wave sound calls us awake.

I walk the shore at night, slim waves
                                    shatter around my feet —

doilies of foam. Overhead: a blinking red airplane.

Water & sky both dark so it's as if there's no horizon —

what Zen masters call non-duality —
the universe without boundaries: moonless,

freckles of star,
                    boat light shimmering dimly below.

I want to write a phenomenology of the wave shattering
& reforming, the phenomenology of light
in orange crests rippled with shadow.

Dawn divides the sky & earth once more, reaffirming
what we know.
                    A local works with homemade lobster traps
wood, mesh & rope,

then drops one offshore, only a homemade buoy marking it
— plastic bleach jug — bobbing so close I could swim there.

I used to watch men at South Beach
laboring with crab traps: hauling the ropes hand over hand,
plucking crustaceans gently
then plopping them in buckets. I'd pause there on the pier
as they harvested,
                some for restaurants, some for dinner.

I'd trot to the pier's end behind my mother's boyfriend,
he who tried to teach the rod & reel,
who tried to chart for me the territories of manhood.

He's disappeared into those years …

I want to write the phenomenolgy of the vanishing
horizon. I want
to write the phenomenology of this self.

How are those two things different?

Early morning rain —
              tropical, torrential —
                            for only a few minutes

then sun converting puddles to steam.

These islands were once magma. I know this.
Liquid to solid/ liquid to gas.

I sweat. I breathe. I can rub my fingers together — sacred truths of
physical science:

no prayer but the solace of facts.

The sharks that crash against the lobster cages
are sometimes pulled up in rope tangles. Some are killed
with a blow to the head,
& served in restaurants to tourists like us;

others are released flopping into the sea again.

I see one swimming in the shoals at dawn —
it returns splashing toward deeper water
as the tide slumps,
     shark gills pumping for breath.

I watch it, silver in the silvery water, till it seems to vanish.
I almost know where it's going.

Notes

"The Lost Letters of Cumberland" is based on actual love letters found.

"Cooking Italian" is in memory of Frances Vesavinci.

"After Breakfast I Consider String Theory"
The epigraph is from the Clash's "London Calling."

"Walking Meditation"
The epigraph is from *The Wholehearted Way*, a translation of Eihei Dōgen's *Bendōwa*. Translated by Shohaku Okumura and Taigen Daniel Leighton.

"Poem Found in the Graffeti on a Freight Train's Cars" is for Samantha Byers. The poem uses lines from Whitman.

"Thinking of the Franciscan Abbey after Reading James Wright" is for Stephen Dunn.

"Walking the Neighborhood the Morning after a Snow Storm" was written using Jim Simmerman's "Twenty Little Poetry Exercises" prompt. It's dedicated to his memory.

About the Author

Gerry LaFemina is the author of five previous collections of poetry, including *Graffiti Heart* (winner of the Anthony Piccione Prize in Poetry), *The Window Facing Winter* and *The Parakeets of Brooklyn* (winner of the Bordighera Prize); two collections of prose poems; and *Wish List*, a collection of short stories. A former punk musician and a former member of the Associated Writing Programs Board of Directors, he directs the Frostburg Center for Creative Writing at Frostburg State University, where he also teaches. He divides his time between Maryland and New York.